BEFORE YOU SAY "I DO" WORKBOOK FOR CHRISTIAN COUPLES

A PREPARATION AND MINDFULNESS GUIDE FOR CHRIST-CENTERED RELATIONSHIPS TO KEEP YOUR MARRIAGE; PRE-MARRIAGE QUESTIONS, EXERCISES AND REFLECTIONS

KIT SILVA

CONTENTS

SPECIAL BONUS!

WANT THIS BOOK FOR FREE?

GET **FREE**, UNLIMITED ACCESS TO IT AND ALL OF MY NEW BOOKS BY JOINING THE FAN BASE!

Scan with your camera to join!

ABOUT THE AUTHOR

My name is Kit Silva. I need to confess: I wish we had a book like this to guide us before we got married. Oh boy, we've learnt a lot along the way, and it didn't always go smoothly. Due to my own struggles, I'm passionate about initiating communication, resolving interpersonal conflicts, and learning effective strategies in my interactions with people. I think it's crucial to impart the knowledge necessary for others to strengthen and reinvigorate their relationships since I have a lot of respect for couples living the example of a long-lasting and fulfilling marriage.

Because of the great respect I have for the commitment of marriage, I'm writing this book. I think that many men and women out there need help in their daily relationship challenges, just like my friends do when they get engaged and prepare to be married. I'd like to share with you the knowledge I've acquired over the years through working with many different kinds of people. My ultimate goal is to help spouses better understand each other's responsibilities, behaviors, and reactions to create stronger relationships and help keep families together.

Through the activities, useful advice, and engaging games in this book, you can travel with me. I want to demonstrate to you that if you put genuine effort into your marriage, the "honeymoon phase" may last indefinitely.

INTRODUCTION

"Therefore shall a man leave his father and his mother, and shall cleave unto his wife: and they shall be one flesh."

— (KING JAMES BIBLE [KJB], 1769/2022, GENESIS 2:24)

You chose to read the *Before you say "I do" Workbook for Christian Couples*, which means that you care a great deal about having a marriage that pleases the Lord. It also means that you're looking for ways to have the best relationship possible with your future spouse. We invite you into this study, where you'll find help with answering and asking tough questions, and lots of fun exercises that will help you get to know your future spouse even better than you already do! In Biblical scripture, you'll find God's confirmation that a house built on rock will stand (Matthew 7:24–25), and the one built on sand won't last long.

The goal of this workbook is to assist you through key building blocks that will help you construct a Christian marriage that will last. When its structure gets cracked, and the winds of life and change hit time and again, it will be steady and able to withstand many storms. Important topics we'll discuss include: God's plan and your plan, the roles of husband and wife in a marriage, intimacy, commitment, raising children, finances, communication, and handling conflict in your relationship.

HOW TO USE THIS WORKBOOK

In this workbook, we'll discuss what God's desires and intentions are for your marriage. We'll have a look at your own desires and intentions as individuals and as a couple. The most important part is to see God's purpose for bringing you together, and adjust your plans to fit in his design for your life together.

Please complete this workbook with your future spouse. The workbook has six sessions or chapters. Try to complete at least one session a week. If possible, spend an hour a day, or put aside a morning or afternoon over the weekend. You'll need to be sure that there are no distractions like future in-laws coming over for coffee! So, what will be expected from you? You'll need to do the following for each session or chapter:

- Read the lesson and complete the exercises together.
- Discuss the answers with your future spouse; and reflect on it.
- Where you identify areas of concern or additional questions, discuss them with a mentor such as your preacher or church group leader.

Pray together throughout your adventure. May this workbook be a building block for your future marriage, and bless your union in all the ways necessary!

1

GOD'S PLAN VERSUS YOUR PLAN

Once you get married, you become a team, but you're not cloned. Two people, in many cases, from diverse backgrounds, different thinking, friendships, habits, and future dreams don't need to change to be married. The secret lies in respecting and supporting one another, and ultimately, this can only be done once you truly understand each other. How will I understand my partner? Through communication and being willing to set aside the time to listen to them. That being said, this is only the tip of the enormous iceberg called marriage. Yes, you heard it right. Marriage is in no way easy! You need to row the boat together to manage the stream. If you're wise enough to know that the boat is steered by God, then you'll be able to row easily through life's storms. How do you incorporate two different people's lives and plans, and above all, make it fit into God's ultimate plan for you as individuals, a couple, and a new family? Let's have a look at valuable advice about God's plan versus your plan.

CENTERING THINGS AROUND GOD'S PLAN

If you're anything like me, you've wondered why some couples seem to have such amazing relationships while others seem to be terribly unhappy. I decided to ask a number of couples who had been married for many years and still liked one another. Many of my married friends shared their biggest secret. So, what was it? They said that if you place Jesus at the center of your marriage, it will work. I found peace in that answer. With Jesus as the core, how could anything go wrong? So, I decided to ask the inevitable question: "How do you make Jesus the center of your marriage?"

Much to my amazement, most of these happy couples couldn't say how. They knew they had done it, but they had never tried to actually figure out the habits they practiced that led them to this important point. Some, though, offered marriage advice based on real-world experiences, which I've found to be incredibly helpful in my own marriage too. Let's have a look at some of the advice that stood out.

How to Discover God's Plan for Your Marriage

Pray about it. Every discussion about making decisions should start with prayer. If anybody among you lacks wisdom, they should ask God, who freely gives to all without finding fault, and it will be given to them, according to James 1:5. The Holy Spirit takes pleasure in sharing God's wisdom with those who are receptive to it.

Speak life into your choices. Check to see if the choices you're going to make will be life-giving. There are so many options in our life, and each one either strengthens or weakens the unity of our marriage. We shall always be guided by the Holy Spirit to make choices that are life-giving. The nature of our decisions is clearly stated in Deuteronomy 30:19 (*KJB*, 1769/2022) which reads: "[...] I have set before you life and death, blessing and cursing: therefore choose life, that both thou and thy seed may live."

To achieve unity, invite the Holy Spirit. Ask the Holy Spirit to guide you both to the same understanding of God's intentions for marriage. Ephesians 4:2–3 (*Holy Bible, New International Version [NIV]*, 1973/2011) instructs us to "be completely humble and gentle [...] Make every effort to uphold the spiritual bond of peace."

Be attentive and quiet. Instead of acting as a channel for what you believe the Holy Spirit wants to say to your spouse, pay attention to what He is trying to tell you.

What type of questions should you be asking the Holy Spirit about? For example, the Holy Spirit's guidance on how technology fits into your marriage is something you should be actively pursuing. There are no scriptures in the Bible that guide us about using text messages, blogs, Facebook, Instagram, Twitter, or Snapchat in our marriages. With these attractive online tools, we don't want to lose the chance to give life to our love, but we also don't want to be easily controlled by something that was only intended to be a tool. We all use social media in different ways, making it easy for us to disagree with one another about suitable amounts and times for use. You should agree on a strategy with your spouse that will give your love more life. Pray, look, and listen together for guidance.

I'm not sure what the Holy Spirit will communicate to you and your spouse, but He has made it clear to me that I ought to take my husband to bed more often than I take my phone! So far, many couples have had great success using these suggestions to put Jesus at the center of their relationship and to carry out God's plan for their marriage.

2

YOUR ROLES AS HUSBAND AND WIFE

Feeling unsure about your future roles? You're definitely not alone. No one knows what to expect from a marriage, and each married couple is uniquely structured as a unit.

Tammy has always been a kind and helpful wife. When Andrew gets home, dinner is always ready, the kids are bathed and ready for bed, and his clothes for the next day are ironed and waiting. He can just take his shoes off and chill out. But the last few weeks have been hard. She doesn't feel like Andrew cares about her, and the fact that he doesn't talk to her after work makes her feel like she's not appreciated. He's too tired to be intimate, and she can't help but wonder if he's in love with someone else.

Andrew comes home exhausted to the core. His company is reorganizing its staff, and he worries that he'll be next to lose his job. How will he tell Tammy if he gets fired from his job? He is the only one in their family who brings in money. Tammy is the best wife he could ask for, and he loves her very much. She takes care of the house and the kids like a pro. He likes how brave and kind she is. He feels bad that he hasn't talked to her in a few weeks, but he doesn't want to worry her or, worse, let her down.

Do you see from these examples how perceptions differ, and how important regular communication is in a marriage?

Can you relate to situations where you were unsure about you or your partner's roles? You'll need to discuss your future expectations from one another before you say *I do* because *I do* means forever.

Life and marriage are both hard for everyone. God's most important message to us is to love each other. But He doesn't leave us to figure out how to do this on our own. His words are full of important lessons that can help us every step of the way. Marriages and families are set up in different ways, and that's okay. This could be by choice or because of circumstances. Still, you might feel less important if you don't contribute to the household income, or your ego might be hurt if you earn less than your spouse.

Think about why you got married and the things that your partner loves about you. Put your weaknesses behind you and show off your strengths! Help and care for each other, and look for ways to make each other's lives easier. In some homes, both men and women work, do chores around the house, and take care of the children. Some men are great at cleaning, while some women are terrible, and the same is true the other way around. Nothing ever happens in the same way in different households. Make your own rules that work for your family based on your situation, the way you live, or how messy your house is. Do not, I repeat, do not ever compare your family, marriage, kids, or home to anyone else's, not even your own parent's example. Live the life that is right for you and don't be like anyone else. That is lovely! If you want to copy some-one's way of living, someone who has been through life and made it out alive, then follow Jesus' example.

"Follow God's example, therefore, as dearly
loved children and walk in the way of love,
just as Christ loved us and gave himself up
for us as a fragrant offering and sacrifice
to God"

— (*NIV*, 1973/2011, EPHESIANS 5:1–2)

If your (future) husband expects you to become a stay-at-home wife, and this is not in your aspirations, you should talk to him honestly about it. He needs you to tell him how you really feel. If you can't handle being a housewife, you should find a job, a side job you can do from home, or a hobby that will meet your needs. Include him in the conversation and let him help you decide what to do. Respect and honor his opinion. In the end, this choice will affect both of you, and it will be a lot easier if he feels respected.

Even when we give a lot of ourselves away because we love others, we still need to love ourselves enough to grow and change as people. Once we've filled our own cups, we'll be able to give our loved ones a drink of life, happiness, and hope.

Dear *man*, don't ignore what your wife wants and needs. Support her feelings, whether she's working and wants to be a stay-at-home wife or the other way around and wants to get a job. If you're a good planner, you could ask her to show you or talk to you about her action plan or business plan for the future. Set aside time to sit down and talk about it. If it's hard for you to show how you feel, set a daily reminder on your phone to tell your wife how much you care about her. Set a reminder to give her the day off, buy her flowers, or run her a bath.

Ephesians 5 is a great guide for both husbands and wives. I think this shows that there has always been a struggle between men and women and that we should pay close attention to each other's needs and feelings when we get married.

Wives, submit yourselves to your own husbands as you do to the Lord. For the husband is the head of the wife as Christ is the head of the church, his body, of which he is the Savior. Now as the church submits to Christ, so also wives should submit to their husbands in everything.

Husbands, love your wives, just as Christ loved the church and gave himself up for her to make her holy, cleansing her by the washing with water through the word, and to present her to himself as a radiant church, without stain or wrinkle or any other blemish, but holy and blameless. In this same way, husbands ought to love their wives as their own bodies. He who loves his wife loves himself. After all, no one ever hated their own body, but they feed and care for their body, just as Christ does the church—for we are members of his body. "For this reason a man will leave his father and mother and be united to his wife, and the two will become one flesh." This is a profound mystery—but I am talking about Christ and the church. However, each one of you also must love his wife as he loves himself, and the wife must respect her husband. (*NIV*, 1973/2011, Ephesians 5:22–33)

3

COMMUNICATION AND CONFLICT

B eing in a marriage has its ups and downs. When you start a family, it's the same. When it tends to come to conflict, it's well known that communication can have a big impact on whether or not a relationship moves forward. Even though the phrase *better and faster* pops up in modern times, it may not be the best way to build a lasting relationship. Some things that couples do together may become so routine that they do them more on autopilot than on purpose, which is great for planes but terrible for relationships. Our minds aren't always in the present, which makes it hard to get to the right level of closeness in our marriages. Contrary to what most people think, slowing down makes people happier overall, including in their relationships. Couples can slow it down by practicing mindfulness, which is about self-reflection, awareness, not being critical, and being active in the moment.

Did you know that one in every three marriages in the U.S. ends in divorce? In today's fast-paced culture, exhaustion, a lack of communication, loneliness, a loss of intimacy, and stress are all things that make it harder for a marriage to work. If you have trouble with any of these, learning how to relax is a great way to make your marriage more satisfying. If you can implement good communication even before commencing with your marriage, all the better!

Quick communication tips to get you thinking about the topic you're about to tackle:

- Let your partner have some space.
- Talk to each other face-to-face
- When things go wrong, use *I* statements, not *you* statements
- Tell the truth.
- Talk about the little things.
- Make sure to follow the 24-hour rule to deal with issues promptly.
- Maintain personal contact (hugs, hands, touch, kiss).
- Keeping interaction fun is best done by making it interesting.

This chapter will show you how to communicate and solve problems in a fun way.

COUPLES' COMMUNICATION ACTIVITIES

Ghost-The-World

We live in a time when there are too many things to take in, and most of us don't get much time to ourselves. It's time to switch the world off. Put your phones in a sealed bag for a predetermined number of hours (decide together, for example, 5 hours) and have a good old-fashioned conversation with your partner. If you're worried about problems at work or home, check your phone once every few hours to see if you missed any important messages or calls. Whether it's cold or warm outside, it can be very nice to get cozy, be quiet, and look up at the night sky. Sometimes, it's nice to see each other in a beautiful place and just be quiet.

Retreat Together

Strengthen your connection with your future spouse by going on a couples' retreat. It's a great way to spend time with your special someone. You could choose from outdoor retreats, going away with friends, religious retreats, etc. Check with your church to find out about pre-wedding group retreats near you. You'll be able to relax and feel happier in your relationship, and you'll also be able to meet other couples who are going through the same thing.

Have an Open Conversation With Your Future Spouse

Since President Roosevelt held *fireside chats* to talk to the American people. The phrase has come to mean love, openness, and a willingness to say anything. This is because the term *fireside chat* makes you think of a nice conversation in front of a warm fire. Pick a comfortable seat for each of you, get a nice drink for each of you, and have a nice chat. Give each other your full attention and don't be afraid to say what's on your mind.

Confess, Apologize, and Fix It

Everyone has a past, and it doesn't take long for one person in a romantic relationship to say something that hurts, criticizes, or puts down the other in some way. Take some time for each of you to quietly bring up one hurtful thing the other said or did so that you can both try to figure out how to say the same thing in a more caring way. This activity is meant to make you feel safe enough to talk about old wounds that you or your partner are still having trouble getting over. The person who made the comment now has a chance to express his or her dissatisfaction or frustration in a different way and apologize for hurting the other person's feelings.

Take Turns Talking

Setting time limits and letting each side talk without being interrupted by the other could be helpful. When it's your turn to listen, don't try to defend or explain anything you said or did that made the other person upset or annoyed. You can also take turns talking about the best parts of your day and one thing that made you feel down. If it's your turn to listen, you can show support, empathy, and compassion without saying a word. But don't say anything until your partner's turn is over. You can each think about what the other person said between your turns. During these meetings, both sides get to say what they want.

Keep a Couple's Journal

Learn each other's love languages and express yourself in those ways. Do you know *The Five Love Languages* books by Dr. Gary Chapman? Each love language describes the ways in which we prefer to give and receive love. Examples of all these include praise spoken aloud, deeds of service, accepting presents, special times spent around each other, and physical contact. Use at least three distinct love languages to present at least three diverse options to one another for a treat. Take turns leaving each other notes in a journal that you both feel at ease using. This journal can be used to express your feelings about anything honestly and passionately without pointing the finger at anyone or passing judgment. Speak to your spouse in a way that doesn't put them on the defensive or cause them to feel excluded by considering how they will respond to what you say. Instead of sharing a journal, you may write letters to each other. Any of these will not only facilitate communication between you and your spouse but will also help both of you become better writers. One example that you could suggest to each other is to give your spouse a long hug and offer to give them a neck massage or a back rub. This is a great opportunity to have your spouse's full attention for at least 30 minutes. The other can enjoy a relaxing bath while the first person cleans the kitchen. A second example is giving a thoughtful gift or surprise based on your spouse's needs. This will build your spouse's confidence with genuine, sincere compliments, etc. You will learn each other's love languages and needs as you practice these types of activities more frequently, which will help you maintain each other's love tanks.

Talk About Your Aspirations and Goals for the Future

If you're married, it's essential that you and your spouse are aware of one another's goals and plans for the next five years or so. Answer the following questions as a couple: What do you really want? Why do you think that would appeal to you? What help can your partner give you? Although it might seem like this is an isolated incident, it isn't. Priorities could change, and the more you develop as a pair, the more probable it is that you will allow instinct to rule your decisions rather than your goals. Additionally, you'll feel closer to one another and get to know one another better the more you understand each other's goals and desires.

Share Lines From the Songs You Like

Even though this might seem like one of those old-fashioned communication games for married couples, it's actually a fun way to learn new things about your partner.

Choose at least one song that you think suits you and say the lyrics that mean the most to you. Have you ever had trouble putting your thoughts into words, but then heard a song that put into words what was going on in your head? Share that song with your partner and ask them to do the same. The goal is to find out how your partner thinks and why certain parts of music are important to them. Best believe, every time you hear that song in future, you'll think of your sweetheart and the time they played it for you.

QUICK COMMUNICATION EXERCISES

Compare your responses to the questions below to determine how well you and your spouse know one another.

About your spouse:

1. What meals does your spouse like to eat?
2. Which one of you is the most dramatic?
3. What kind of outdoor activity does your partner prefer?
4. What book is your partner's favorite?
5. Who is your partner's preferred superhero?
6. What color is your partner's favorite?
7. Which time of year does your partner prefer?
8. What sport does your partner like to watch the most? Are you up for a game?
9. Which restaurant is your partner's favorite?
10. What time of day is preferred by your partner, and why?
11. Your lover dislikes what day of the week, and why?

12. What about other people really irritates your partner?
13. Does your lover enjoy spending time with friends or being alone?
14. What is the first thing your partner will save if your house is on fire?
15. Which pet is preferred by your partner: dogs or cats?

About you:

1. What is the best way for me to express my love? Gifts? Touch? Random acts of generosity? Or, being together for a while?
2. What is the best way for me to receive love?
3. Do you believe I am more of an extrovert or an introvert?
4. Why do I use the word *argument*?
5. What do I like to talk about at the end of the day?
6. Is it possible for me to identify my feelings quickly?
7. What frustrates me the most about my partner, and why?
8. What frustrates my partner the most about me, and why?
9. What can I do to be a better listener?

10. What are my talents and how can I use them to support my partner?

Important questions to ask your future spouse:

1. Do you believe in God?
2. Are you connected to Christ?
3. What does marriage mean to you?
4. How do you think a husband and wife should treat each other? Discuss these roles.
5. How will you treat people who hurt you in some way?
6. Do you want kids, and what are your thoughts on parenting?
7. How important is being honest in your relationships?
8. Where do you think you fall short as a partner?
9. What scares you the most?
10. How important do you think money and possessions are?

CONFLICT IN YOUR MARRIAGE

Avoid unhealthy confrontation. Most divorces have these things in common : disrespect, criticism, defensiveness, and *stonewalling* (Gottman Institute). Don't use these in your marriage. Refrain from using *you* statements, and use *I* statements to get your feelings across. Be willing to listen to your spouse, and respect their feelings even if you don't always agree with them.

Conflict can't be avoided; it's bound to happen in every marriage. The choice lies in how you decide to handle it, and being effective in knowing, compromising, and accepting personal differences. Make sure you're both calm before engaging in discussion.

4

INTIMACY AND COMMITMENT

INTIMACY IN YOUR MARRIAGE

It's simple right? Fall in love, stay in love? You guessed it, that's the toughest part! How do you keep a relationship interesting? Have you ever looked at your marriage and thought, "Is this all there is?" What happens after the honeymoon is over, the house is bought, and the kids are born? Life can get boring when you do the same things every day. Passion is often taken away by mediocrity. And often, the ship is slowly sinking, but we don't realize it until we start to feel like roommates with our partner or like we've completely stopped loving them. But there are ways to keep things interesting in a relationship.

So how do we keep our marriage alive? How do you keep your marriage's fire burning? More than that, how do you stoke passion and desire in your marriage for years to come?

A Narrow View of Marriage

We don't learn in college how to keep a relationship interesting. I think that when it comes to marriage and love, we often settle for less than what's possible. A lot of this has to do with the world we live in. There's little to no pressure from the outside to stay married. Most people say that marriage is hard work and that the excitement should end somewhere. A bad patch in a relationship might as well be a stop sign if you choose it to be. This is the expected norm, so most have no reason to aim their sights higher. And without many great role models, it's easy to agree with this mindset. But that is just what it is—a mindset. And any thought or belief can be redefined or changed according to what you want and choose in life.

Rewrite Your Story

The first step to making a marriage stronger is to stop thinking that it can't work. We need to change what we think marriage is all about in terms of love, passion, desire, and being able to keep those things. Change your story to say, "I won't settle for a loveless, boring marriage. I will do whatever it takes to keep my relationship fresh." When you have the right attitude, good things will happen in your relationship, because

"For as he thinketh in his heart, so is he"

— (KJB, 1769/2022, PROVERBS
23:7).

Keeping a Marriage Interesting Takes Work

Intention is everything. Being intentional is the key to getting the marriage of your dreams. To know how to keep a relationship fresh, you have to be very clear on what you want, what you know is possible, and what will be needed to get there. Here are some things you can start doing right now to start making your marriage stronger:

- **Learn the basics.** It's important to know what your partner thinks about passion, romance, and love. Learn how to love them in a way that they'll enjoy. Know how they want to be loved, what bugs them, and what they need. Learn about their fears, hopes, and doubts.
- **Always be there.** Presence means paying full attention when you talk to your spouse; being fully there when you show love, and giving

your best at all times. There is never a time when you aren't trying to make your marriage as loving as you want it to be, and nothing is ever more important than that. That doesn't mean that you don't use your attention and time in other parts of your life. It means that your marriage is more important than the other things you do with your time and energy.

- **Set a goal.** To keep a relationship interesting, you need to have a clear idea of where you want your marriage to be and set goals that you can measure. Keep track of how you're doing.

- **Check in with your spouse:** at least once a week. Set aside at least one evening a week for this. Both sides should be able to talk about their worries, frustrations, or areas where they think things could be better without being judged or told they are wrong. Conversation should be about getting closer and making more connections. This is the time to measure where both partners feel the marriage is at and determine what you can both do to serve each other better and resolve any conflicts.

- **Yes, indeed. Believe it!** You can have a dream marriage! There are many more things that can be done to keep the marriage fresh, but if you use these few steps and make them a part of your everyday life, it will make a big difference in your marriage. If you think your marriage has reached a dead end, think about what story you've been telling yourself about it and what new story you could tell yourself instead. If you change the way you think, your marriage will be stronger than ever.

LOVE AND COMMITMENT

The one thing you can count on hearing at a wedding— 1 Corinthians 13, which speaks all about love. It's quoted so frequently, on coffee mugs, jewelry, and even fridge magnets, that they practically qualify as clichés. The thing is, 1 Corinthians 13 is so lovely and profound that it deserves to be heard over and over again. It's a chapter that is applicable to more than just your wedding. Here's how to have a marriage that isn't just a Corinthians wedding verse.

Love is patient, love is kind. It does not envy, it does not boast, it is not proud. 5 It does not dishonor others, it is not self-seeking, it is not easily angered, it keeps no record of wrongs. 6 Love does not delight in evil but rejoices with the truth. 7 It always protects, always trusts, always hopes, always perseveres.

*Love never fails. But where there are prophe-
cies, they will cease; where there are
tongues, they will be stilled; where there is
knowledge, it will pass away.*

— (*NIV*, 1973/2011, 1 CORINTHIANS
13:4–8)

What relevance do these lines have for your marriage in the world today? Let's examine this well-known wedding verse from the book of Corinthians in detail to see how it relates to the debate over what God's definition of love is and isn't.

Love Is Patient

The Corinthians chapter refers to patience in one of its most well-known passages. This is an important lesson to apply to marriage too. Because while patience is undoubtedly necessary in all relationships, it is especially crucial to the health and durability of a marriage.

There will undoubtedly be conflicts and tense situations when two people share a house. However, practicing patience helps ease the annoyance or tension that comes with certain circumstances (e.g., recognizing that life is about growth [not perfection], respecting personal limits and differences, etc.). Additionally, adopting a patient attitude rather than a perfectionism-driven one helps avoid bitterness, which is the death knell for every marriage.

Love Is Kind

In a marriage, a little bit of kindness goes a long way. When two individuals love each other well enough to decide to spend the rest of their lives together, kindness is usually assumed or taken for granted. It's not used as often, though. Because of this, many marriages start to lose both their spark and their shared sense of admiration. They start disliking each other and some even get bitter towards one another. Most people would say "not in that way" when asked if they still love each other. Most of the time, that addendum is caused by not being kind or, more specifically, by a lot of emotional neglect, harshness, constant criticism, or even abuse. Love, on the other hand, is none of these. It's nice. Kind acts must be done every day for a marriage to be happy and successful.

Love Keeps No Record of the Past

The day you get married is the beginning of the rest of your lives as a team. In that way, it's like starting over— the first day of the rest of your life. Use this fact and 1 Corinthians 13 to remind yourself that keeping score in a marriage is a big no-no. Mostly, this makes it impossible to forgive or grow as a person. A person can't get better if they are constantly reminded of the things they did wrong in the past.

Love allows every day to be a new one. When the sun sets and clears away the events of the day, so too should love allow for a clean slate upon sunrise.

Love Protects, Trusts, Hopes, and Perseveres

Even when these steps aren't easily falling into place or it's clear there's work to do to re-instill love in its truest form, this is one bit of Corinthians wedding advice to employ; even when you don't like each other, respect the relationship as a separate entity. In other words, even when acts of love are lacking and patience is running thin with your spouse, express love toward your marriage itself.

This decision protects your relationship—something love also does. Additionally, it's the relationship equivalent of boarding up the windows in preparation for a storm. So, in that way, it's perseverance in its purest form. This helps keep hope alive for a brighter day and employs the trust you'll need in one another to do the work needed to carry that hope into fruition.

If nothing else, when it comes to your marriage and the Biblical reminders of the importance of love and its true definition, remember that love simply is. As such, let it be.

5

FINANCES

G uess what the number one thing that married couples argue about is? Yes, it's money, honey! In these trying times, more couples than ever before are starting their marriage with debt. When you and your partner don't talk openly about money, it can feel like you're carrying the stress and burden all by yourself. When you're honest and have a conversation, you don't just talk about money. You're telling each other about your hopes, dreams, and values, which can make your relationship stronger. You may owe money, but you surely owe it to your spouse to be honest about your situation, even if your marriage contract does not obligate you to do so!

When you talk about money with your spouse, you learn a lot more about them. When you talk about it, you share your worries, dreams, future goals, and a lot more—bringing you closer together. When you're getting closer to a serious relationship, and especially when you're married, it's important to talk about these things. One way to do this is to make a budget together for each month. It gives you a chance to talk about specific financial details you wouldn't have talked about otherwise. When it comes to talking about money, you have to be deliberate, and your life together will be better because of it.

So, it's clear that money is important, but it's not always okay to talk about it, especially when you're just getting to know someone. But if you plan to get married, talking about money is a priority! It can be scary to talk about it. A good place to start is to talk about how money worked in your family when you were growing up, or to share your worries about it. You'll find out a lot about your individual approaches to handling it. You should talk about your future expectations and limitations.

People's approaches towards spending and saving money differ. You'll need to embrace your differences. When it comes to money, everyone will have both strong and weak points. One person might save money and the other might spend it. One may use money sparingly and the other could be an impulsive spender.

Each needs the other to keep things in check. The saver can help the spender set limits, and the spender can remind the saver that it's okay to have fun sometimes. It's neither right nor wrong to be a natural spender or saver. There is no way to be *right*. What matters most is that you plan things together.

Before you get married, you can set yourself up for a good marriage if you talk about your money and plans. Try setting up a budget for a wedding as a practice run. That's a good way to start. Just don't give in to the urge to combine your money before you say *I do*. Don't combine your bank accounts until you're married, and don't pay off your partner's debts before you're married. Although trust is key in a relationship, they also say "don't count your chickens until they have hatched!"

Whatever your approach is for the future, try to avoid incurring new debt as far as possible! Remember, before you can serve others, and give to your community, etc. you need to assure that you're on a clean page with your own financial situation. You cannot serve from an empty cup!

6

RAISING CHILDREN

Congratulations! Most likely, you are reading this chapter because you and your partner are thinking about starting a family someday. The majority of people convey the idea that having children is the ultimate level of being content and joyful. Not as often mentioned is the fact that all of your emotions—not just the good ones—will get stronger. Sleep deprivation, irritability, and maybe feelings of resentment toward the partner who gets to go to work or the one who gets to stay home can lead to arguments and feeling frustrated in your marriage. You might experience anxiety or postpartum depression. As new parents, we experience a range of emotions especially during the first year.

Did you know that, typically, the first three years of parenting cause a significant decrease in marital satisfaction? John Gottman's research found that 67% of couples experience decreased marital satisfaction after having their first child (Carrère et al., 2000). At first, it seems a little weird to think that having children will make you like your partner less. You did have a child with them after all, proving how much you loved them. But when you take into account everything that happens to you during that first year of parenthood, such as the chronic lack of sleep, the challenges with feeding, the lack of energy, lack of intimacy, and the fact that you are primarily trying to use logic with a tiny human being who hasn't yet developed logic, it becomes quite clear why that first year is so difficult.

There's no specific fail-proof recipe to follow when it comes to raising kids. The best course of action is to tailor your solutions to your particular family system because families come in many shapes and sizes with diverse backgrounds and ideologies. However, the tips below will help you embrace and survive your new reality.

Schedule time to talk. It's not the right moment to discuss significant differences in your parenting styles with your partner when you're busy taking care of your infant or in front of your children as they get older. Set aside some time to talk about the issues when both of you are at ease and free from interruptions or kids.

Keep your expectations practical. People will tell you all the time how lovely being a parent is, and they are right. However, people sometimes downplay the amount of work and stress needed to keep the baby alive throughout that first year. You shouldn't expect your child to speak in complete phrases or even routinely sleep through the night during the first year. All of those things are wonderful ideals, but for many families, they are not the reality. So, try to have reasonable or even low expectations.

The most reasonable goal is survival for everyone on board. I know that seems absurd, but if your only goal for the first year is survival, you'll feel accomplished and proud of yourself when it's through.

It's not forever. Whatever occurs throughout the first year of having a baby is only a temporary situation. It doesn't matter if the infant has a cold, doesn't sleep through the night, or if you feel like you haven't left your house in days. Keep in mind that these trying times will pass. You'll ultimately be able to leave the house and start sleeping through the night again. Even better, one day you'll be able to have dinner with your partner while your child is still awake and calmly playing in the living room! You only need to have patience because the good days will return.

Find reasons to celebrate. Find activities that you both enjoy doing with your child, and take lots of pictures. When your child no longer requires you, those images of joyful occasions will be treasured. Those pictures will also be treasured when you need a little pick-me-up to remind yourself that you're doing a wonderful job.

How we take care of ourselves changes when we have our first child. At first, pampering yourself might not mean going to the spa, going on dates, or sleeping in. Especially talking to the ladies, self-care changes when you have a new child. Even things like eating, sleeping, taking a shower, and going to the bathroom become luxuries. Try to do what those simple rules say. Try to take at least one shower a day. During your infant's naps, sleep. I know that if you follow this piece of advice, you'll be annoyed because you'll be thinking, "Well, when am I going to clean, do dishes, and cook meals?" The problem is that all of these things change when you become a parent. It's okay to get takeout for dinner, have a messy house, and buy new underwear from Amazon because you didn't have time to do the laundry. Get as much sleep and rest as you can because they are as important as air. Make time for your spouse, even if it's a quick cup of coffee while the baby is asleep. Your spouse will appreciate having time with you.

Ask for help. I know that you don't want to look like a burden or needy in social situations, but the first year of being a parent is different. Just say "yes, please" when people ask for help. When they ask, "What should we bring?" be honest. I've asked family members who are coming over for the party to bring dinner, friends to stop by Target and get more pacifiers, and my mother-in-law to watch my twins so I can take a shower in peace. Accept all the help you can get! No one ever said anything bad to me about it either. Especially in the first year, most people want to help you.

I hope that these little bits of advice will help you and your partner get through the first year of being a parent. I have two-year-old twins—a boy and a girl—so I know how hard the first year is. You'll face problems you didn't expect, but time goes by quickly, and there are simple things you can do to make your first year of parenting a good one. When you're a parent, the days can feel like they last forever, but the years go by fast.

CONCLUSION

PRE-MARRIAGE COACHING

Before being married, people usually try their hardest, and there are rarely any overt indications that a marriage would end in disagreement. Yet, learning about each other's peculiarities after marriage can be a shocking surprise. Premarital coaching can be very beneficial in identifying the underlying causes of future relationship issues and finding solutions before they snowball into more difficult challenges after marriage.

Premarital counseling is a fantastic technique to assist couples in getting ready for marriage. It increases your chances of having a happy, long-lasting marriage and helps you and your spouse have a strong, healthy relationship. It aids in your overall marital preparedness and gets you ready for a beautiful future together.

Finding a counselor you can trust and who respects your particular situation is crucial if you want to get outstanding pre-marriage guidance and ideas. Every day, new pre-marriage counseling models and techniques are being developed, encouraging the bride and groom to build solid, healthy relationships before getting married. It imparts to the couple the knowledge and abilities required to lay a solid, conscious basis for their union. Share a faith-based connection through dedication, trust, effort, and the enthusiasm to build a successful marriage!

Last Take-Home Thoughts

You must be 100% certain that you're prepared for this lifelong journey before entering into a marriage. Making preparations for marriage is essential for a strong and successful partnership. Knowing yourself, your strengths, weaknesses, hobbies, values, and expectations is crucial. Out of this information, the question arises: Are you truly prepared for marriage and to freely and joyfully share your life with your spouse?

REFERENCES

Believe Guest Contributor. (2019, January 29). *Expert insights: Talking about money in a relationship.* Believe by Christian Mingle. https://www.christianmingle.com/en/believe/love/relationships/talking-about-money

Carrère, S., Buehlman, K. T., Gottman, J. M., Coan, J. A., & Ruckstuhl, L. (2000). Predicting marital stability and divorce in newlywed couples. *Journal of Family Psychology, 14*(1), 42–58. https://doi.org/10.1037/0893-3200.14.1.42

Gottman, J. (March, 2000). *Marriage and couples - Research.* The Gottman Institute. https://www.gottman.com/about/research/couples/

Holy Bible, New International Version (NIV). (2011). Biblica Online.

https://www.biblica.com/online-bible/ (Original work published 1973)

King James Bible. (2022). King James Bible Online. https://www.kingjamesbibleonline.org/ (Original work published 1769)